Eternal Sparrow

Poetry for love, laughter and life

by

Ingrid Collins

Strategic Book Publishing
New York, New York

Strategic Book Publishing
An imprint of AEG Publishing Group
845 Third Avenue, 6th Floor - 6016
New York, NY 10022
www.StrategicBookPublishing.com

ISBN: 978-1-60860-535-4

Printed in the United States of America

Illustrated by Giovanna Cellini

Book Design: SP

Dedication

To my husband, Malcolm "Nick"; my mother, Mona;
the memory of my late father, Jack;
and to the love we share.

Acknowledgements

My heartfelt thanks go to my illustrator, Giovanna Cellini, for creating breathtakingly beautiful images, distilling the spirit of my work like the visual equivalent to haikus; my gratitude also goes to the wonderfully professional editorial team at Strategic for all their help and advice in the creation of this book.

Table of Contents

7

8

Preface

Poetry has always been a delight for me. Words, when accurate, resonate and roll deliciously around my mind's mouth. As a child, I remember gasping at the brilliance of the poet Gerard Manley Hopkins, who could write lines like "For skies of couple-color as a brindled cow / For rose moles all in stipple upon trout that swim," and Shakespeare, who wrote "Love is not love that alters when it alteration finds / Or bends with the remover, to remove," amongst his one or two other jottings.

The title of this anthology, *Eternal Sparrow,* refers to my sonnet about the power of a poem to carry the voice of the poet through the millennia, to collapse the dimensions of time, distance, and cultures and connect heart to heart, soul to soul with the reader. I do not have the temerity to compare myself to Caius Valerius Catullus, whose poem on the death of Lesbia's pet sparrow inspired me: *"Passer mortuus est meae puellae, / Passer, deliciae meae puellae, / Quam plus illa oculis suis amabat: / Nam mellitus erat, suamque norat / Ipsam tam bene quam puella matrem."*

I do love a challenge, and so I have attempted to express myself using form poetry structures of varying varieties of draconian difficulty. I remember that the shadow of the sestina loomed large on my fear list until I had written one of my own and had therefore tamed it until it could nibble the words gently out of my hand like a friendly horse accepting a sugar lump delicately, warmly, with his velvety muzzle. Poetry is such a personal taste, isn't it? Of the literary friends I admire and to whom I have apprehensively shown my work, the comments have ranged from enthusiastically flattering and extremely complimentary to, "But, Ingrid, *darling,* this is *so* nineteenth century!"

Poetry to me is like our two Burmilla cats, Tui & Magic: elegant, graceful, meditative, focused, emotional, beautiful, fabulously representative of the natural world, at times playful and sometimes surprisingly, supremely silly. I am not an academic poet; I have no aspirations to be profound or obscure. I do not write for other poets and have no delusions of grandeur that my work is anything other than communicative, accessible, entertaining, and hopefully substantive enough to distinguish it from the greeting card doggerel form. I started writing poetry as a hobby, and it turned into a passion that often keeps me awake into the early hours of most mornings. I was born and live in England, so I write in British English rather than American English; and I am sure that my American readers are intelligent enough to translate some variations in the spellings. George Bernard Shaw said, "America and England are two countries divided by the same language." I hope the ideas and emotional messages in my poetry translate easily and unite us.

All my love poems are for my husband, Nick. We met in 1970, and we have been laughing and loving ever since. It is he who has inspired me to create this anthology. He is my lover, my friend, my hero, my supporter, my constructive critic, and at times my healer.

So, what will you think of my anthology, I wonder? I offer it with some trepidation and a great measure of joy as well. To send my poems out into the world, like my grandfather used to release the wild birds he had nursed back to health, to send them flying from my imagination and into the blue on their journey to you—this is exciting, but the effort and the courage needed has been massive. I have enjoyed the discipline of attempting to adhere to the rigour of rhythms, the idiosyncratic pulses as in iambic pentameters, the stern strictures of sonnets, and the high art of haikus. Please treat them with care, amusement, and curiosity; and if they should bring you pleasure, please write and let me know?

Ingrid Collins
London, 18th November 2008

Eternal Sparrow

Two thousand years ago a tiny bird

Loved by a Roman beauty met his death.

Catullus, poet, was by passion stirred

And penned light lines, as fresh as baby's breath.

"She loved him more than her own eyes," wrote he,

"For he was gentle." Furthermore, he told

Of their affection pure that held the key

To sacred love, precious to her as gold.

That sparrow and his mistress live anew,

In everlasting, perfect adoration.

Catullus told their tale. There's no adieu

And their true bond still offers inspiration.

Thus poems can send echoes throughout time

And touch our hearts today with love sublime.

Sestina: Reflections on Healing

beauty, love, courage, healing, joy, soul

I live for love of life, a life of beauty,
For wonderful is life that lets me love.
In relegating fear and choosing courage,
I offer to my friends my gift of healing,
And in the act of giving feel such joy
That I become elated in my soul.

In remedying illness, 'tis the soul
In search of peace, in search of truth and beauty,
That will not rest until it finds real joy,
That bliss that comes when feeling profound love.
This is the true intent of spiritual healing:
We conquer inner fears with faith and courage.

So for this quest we face the foe with courage.
The foe? Our fear it is that hurts the soul.
Medical doctors give our bodies healing
But oft they miss the spirit's need for beauty,
And medicine is no substitute for love.
What tincture can deliver total joy?

Before most illness, there's a loss of joy.
This sense of loss we tackle with great courage.
Instinctively we reach out for the Love
We know, deep in our hearts, will cure the soul.
We also realize that thoughts of beauty
Will help to speed the process of our healing.

So many seek to own the gift of healing,
But healing has no ego—there's the joy!
When bringing healing from the world of beauty,
(The Realm, where spirit messengers give courage
To nourish faltering hope), God feeds the soul
And He restores our sense of awe and love.

Before there's life, there has to exist love.
For God is love, and He the fount of healing.

The wonder and awareness in the soul
Brings happiness to warm our world with joy,
To banish sadness and the lack of courage,
Choosing gladness, laughter, light, and beauty.

Whilst we give love, experiencing joy,
We offer service, healing, and good courage.
Entire then is the soul. Great is God's beauty!

Haiku: From the Chrysalis

Butterfly's wings dry
In the hot summer sunshine.
Welcome maturity.

Perhaps

Perhaps I might have lived before?
A smuggler bold with contraband,
A peasant poor in days of yore,
Or lady in a foreign land?

Were you with me, and did we fly
As brother, father, daughter, wife?
Did you and I in days gone by
Play out a great dramatic life?

Together did we feel this force,
This love that shines now with such bliss,
As cat or horse (or mouse, of course)?
And did we fight, or only kiss?

Our partnership, with facets bright
That send out rays that dazzle so,
Emits such light, attains such height,
That truly I'm intrigued to know.

However many lives, begun
A million times, I'd still prove true.
A rich man's son, fish, bird, or nun,
I'd only sing love's song to you.

Anticipation

Glowering heavens, ponderous, intense
With weighty, cumbersome charcoal clouds,
Drawing close enough to touch,
Deeply sigh with promise.
Profound luminosity emanates
From the garden's green soul
And colours, blossoms' pure power,
Of carmine, cobalt, and gold
Compete for the observer's eye,
Eager as young teens at their first school hop.
Hush! The bumble bee, preoccupied, flies low,
Returning to the haven of his hive
To dance beware messages for his eager swarm.
Click-clack of cat flap heralds the return,
From arabesques and jetées with doomed butterflies
On daisied lawn, of pampered feline
To her cushion-comfortable bed.
Small bird secretly huddles, silent in hidden nest,
Occasional soft chirrups the sole clue
Highlighting her apprehensive heart.
I, too, am still, breathless, mindful, rapt,
Revelling in expectation of clattering thunder,
And wide-wakening, illuminating lightning
That reveals all mighty mountains, luscious meadows,
Immense oceans and sweeping sky with electric clarity.
O how I luxuriate in the excitement of this moment,
Hand in hand with you, heart full of wonder,
Before the imminent, soaking celebration
Of the urgent storm.

Haiku: On a Lake in Ise, Japan

and the peace I found there

Circles in water;
Tall reeds give sanctuary
To the golden carp.

15

Translation of a Latin poem

At the cave mouth, poppies grow
And other flowers that bestow
A restful sleep on those below—
On Earth—who toil and labour so;
Dark clouds glide silently around,
A swirling mist seeps through the ground;
No dawn comes here, no sun's ray bright
Enters this realm of endless night.
No gentle breezes do bestir
The branches, and the dewy air
Is filled with dreams. These phantom things
Throughout the cave on gossamer wings
Are drifting, floating, hov'ring round.
Now, from beneath a rock, the sound
Of a gently flowing river,
Tributary of Lethe, ever
Bringing sweet forgetfulness
In dreams.
Upon his couch with deepening sighs,
And peaceful heart and shaded eyes,
Somnus, ancient god of sleep,
Resting in a slumber deep
Reigns over all.

Sonnet: On Love and Fear

Sing of the glorious end of darkening fear.

And hasten perfect love and golden laughter!

We have no time to dwell on darkness drear,

Nor will to build sad memories hereafter.

When love's our monarch, we then to the light

Do turn. Within the heav'nly glow divine,

Perceived as sacred, beauteous, and bright,

All's seen in its true form and honest line.

So let the heavy bonds of grieving fall away,

Let's choose bright sunlight and a loving kiss.

What ecstasy! Come, on this wondrous day,

And celebrate our unity in bliss.

Thus to the world let our brave legacy remain:

Our love and courage vanquish'd fear and pain.

Cyril Casimir. In Memoriam

Mute grave stands in hallowed purpose;
Silent stone sentinel in time's sands
Over your soul loquacious:
Eternity erases
Tattered remembrance of earthly status
At life's ending.
How certain then Time's lance

Shattered the kernel impermanence
Of a name.
In the doctor's art,
Here's milk of being human, kind,
To ease the agitated mind:
Here's value eternal in the pure intending
And the true heart,
Connecting through curiosity,
With no thought abiding of worldly fame.
You served with clarity and dedication,
With wit, intelligence,
With humour o'erriding,
With professional diligence
With focus on your honest soul's
Foundation.
In your medical vocation and healing role
Always ethical.
You were not, however, practical.
Do you recall
The time you tried to open wide
A carton of milk, and spilt it all?
Then our shoulders shook
With hilarious, resounding mirth—
Pure comic book!
"No use crying over spilt milk!"
We laughed with you
In milk-soaked state.
Now we remember you,
Mourn for you, and celebrate
Your worth.
And I'm sure your spirit hears
This spilling now is not of humankindness' milk,
Just tears.

The Magic Roundabout

The merry fairground carousel fades,
Vanishes into time's dark shades.
See, we have grown too sane—
And old!

So many seasons' sun and rain
And tears
Upon our ageing cheeks,
Decades flow from years
And weeks.
Ah! How we forget to ride
Astride
The painted horses, lingering still
In childhood dreams,
It seems,
Where our young hopes
Abide.
Such peppermint-striped,
Cotton-candy innocence will
Hurdygurdily whirl again,
Should we but choose
The overhyped
But iridescent, delicious,
Affectionate recollection
Of our youthful
Existence.

Haiku: My Neighbour, the Blackbird

What pure intention
Greater than that of the bird
That sings to Heaven?

The Thief

From my kitchen window, I see
A squirrel laughing in the lime tree.
He's stolen my strawberries flagrantly!
Now I'll not have any for my tea.

Can anyone use a spare carton of cream?

The Cockerel, the Dragon, and the Worm.

To all those who think telling others what to do is a good idea

In times of legend, once there was
A cockerel bold, whose dragon friend
Was jealous of him. This because
His horns the cockerel wouldn't lend.
Let me explain: We know, for sure,
That just horn'd creatures are allowed
To go each night and make a tour
Of Heav'n, to party on a cloud.
In olden times the cockerel did
Have wondrous horns, but his sad pal
The dragon, such an envious kid,
Had none, and to that carnival,
That heavenly party, he yearned to go!
The dragon begged and pleaded, till
The cockerel tired of saying "NO!"
In truth t'was making him quite ill.
And so the cockerel told the worm,
Who every creature knew was wise,
That he was feeling quite infirm.
The worm replied, "You should revise
Your harsh opinion; he's your friend.
He only wants to go one night
To Heaven. I don't comprehend
Why you don't think that it's alright!"
"You're right," the cockerel said. "I've been
A lousy friend. He's promised that
It's only for one night. How mean
Of me, behaving like a brat."
And so the cockerel freely gave
The dragon his horns, and off he flew.
His friend, the dragon, was a knave.
He bade the cockerel "Adieu!"
And so he stayed high in the cloud
Forever after. That is why
Each morning you will hear a loud
And plaintive, angry, piercing cry
As Cockerel shouts up to the blue,
"Oh, give me back what's truly mine!"

20

That's why, as well, a dragon you
Now never see: he's drinking wine
In Heav'n. So the cockerel sad,
When his laments have run their term,
And if he still is feeling bad,
Why then, he turns and EATS THE WORM!!!!

Points of View

"Don't jump up on our dining table!"
We scold our companion cat.
"Don't clutter up my lookout platform
With your dishes,"
Retorts the majestic animal.
"The words we use
Are functional,"
She patiently continues
"And there is no
Objective reality,
Simply your human
Perspective—
Which you naturally seek
To privilege over mine."

Haiku: When Leaves Have Fallen

Lacy finger'd trees,
Winter-silent in the mist
Greet the dawn's faint glow.

Haiku: Reflections in Motion

Moonlight on ocean
And the bright surface dances:
Silent devotion.

Secret Lives of Living Things

I was talking to a man
called Rupert Sheldrake.
He had met in Manhattan
an African Grey Parrot
called Alex,
who, when taught vocabulary
by his owner, Aimee,
could hold a conversation,
not just mimic what he hears
parrot fashion.
Alex can also pick up on
Aimee's thoughts—
speak them to her,
with parrot passion.
This is a weird
but wonderful
bird.

I was talking to a man
called Cleveland Baxter
who proved that
every living thing can
read our thoughts—
so be careful what you think
in the company of your cat
and houseplant.
Never say "Boo!"
To African violets.
Cleve says they're far too sensitive,
get shocked and faint easily,
can flatline for weeks!
They are weird
but wonderful
plants.

I was talking to a presence
called Creation,
who tells me that
we are all one nano-part
of the same, perfect,
entire

whole.
If you hurt any of us,
we all suffer.
If you love any one of us,
we all thrive.
If you offer a kind thought,
we all grow straight and strong
towards the sun,
be we a bird, a plant, an animal, or
human.
We are weird
but wonderful
Beings.

<u>The Ant</u>

In the wistful breeze,
between the dandelions
and the silent burrowing workers
I watch, entranc'd, a plump black ant
scurrying with focus
and intense compulsion,
offering to its species
its contribution;
No thought of self, beyond a drive
for self-preservation
and procreation;
No less divine a being
than the deep philosopher,
watchful poet, king majestic,
industrious housewife.
Whilst there is so much
seductively
to distract my human heart,
how can I lose myself
in thoughts for others' good?
I vow, I must abandon
ego
in emulation of the humble
ant,
and dedicate myself
to my human
community.

Haiku: Autumn Song

Brown-gold leaf falling
Upon the rich and moist earth
As Autumn triumphs

Haiku: Timeless, with Blue Sky

Sea, sky, clouds pass by;
Time and distance, all is one
In the stratosphere.

Haiku: Feline Friends

Graceful elegance,
Sharp, sheath'd claws and furry purrs—
I adore my cats....

Messages in Water

I recently when shopping bought a
Riveting, groundbreaking book
'Bout hidden properties of water—
I'd love for you to take a look!
With magnetic resonance photo
And explanations that entice,
A man, Dr. Masaru Emoto,
Makes images of crystals, ice,
Dividing his samples into two—
To the first, tells something nice;
To the second, says a curse he knew.

Crystals resulting from the first
Gave beauteous patterns to the eye.
(It would be great for quenching thirst.)

The second, I would surely die
If I imbibed those ugly forms!
And so emotion overrules
Physical structure and the norms
Relating to water molecules.

We all know that we are made,
As all life is, with water pure—
Each lovely creature, blossom, blade
Of grass. I wonder, could we cure
Our ills by thinking thoughts serene
And positive, with love in mind?
So that our body's water clean
Away afflictions of all kind?

Emotions influence and form us.
The implications are enormous!

Welcome

A child's love is stronger,
More touching and lighter
Than any precious ornament,
Or pretty adornment.
It lasts longer,
Goes deeper, burns brighter,
So I cherish this precious
And wonderful gift.
I won't let it perish.

A child's laughter is louder,
More perfumed than powder,
More bell-like and musical
Than any sweet symphony
Or solo recital,
Its resonance more profound.
Such gentle harmony!
Its echoes rebound,
Welcome and vital.

Ode to the Mountain Ash

Outside my window, there's a Mountain Ash
Whose supple branches greet the merry breeze.
She catches and flings back the sun's bright flash.
She simply is the loveliest of trees!

The Winter strips her of her pretty leaves,
And bravely in the frost she does survive.
With gentle Spring she wakens and believes
She can recover, and her soul can thrive.

And thus her pretty leaves, by day and night,
Emerge into the world and flutter there,
Now yellow-green she offers to the light,
And curtseys to the stars and the sweet air.

In Summer's warm embrace she stands erect.
She's now attired in emerald green dress.
This little tree the sunshine does reflect
And is the source of such great happiness!

But oh, in Autumn, my dear little tree
With bronze, brown, red, and gold is all aflame!
A ballerina now, most certainly,
She laughs and dances and enjoys her fame.

For I have whispered to her that I've penned
Some lines to her and to her beauty sweet.
I know for sure that she can comprehend.
I thank the Lord that she is in my street!

Amaryllis

For Helen

Three flowers she gave to me
She wanted to say thanks.
I gave my friend what I could give,
Out of the love I had for her
And for our shared history.
I didn't bring healing
To win her plaudits, but she gave me
Amaryllis.
Vermillion blossoms trumpet
Around my kitchen now.
Reminding me of her gratitude.
Three stout stems, so sexy
In my kitchen, saying thanks.
See, how the daylight plays
Over the flame red,
Orange red, burning red,
Iridescence of the petals,
Four to each stem.
She knew it would work, the healing.
I hoped it would, too,
Was blissful when it did.
Not for the "thank you's"
Not for the sturdy amaryllis,
But for friendship and the glory
Of Spirit.

The Nurturing of Birds

My granddad, Eli, loved birds in the wild.
Mother recalls, when she was a small child,
He nursed the injured, mended, set them free.
How he would laugh and chuckle gleefully
As to the clouds his erstwhile captives flew
With strong, bright wings to sing their songs anew.
When, on long winter evenings, she grew bored,
He'd give her pen and paper, to record
How many were there of those souls in flight—
Kept her attention busily though the night,
For those small, feathered spirits can't keep still!
And now, today, I think it is God's will
That grandad's soul still cares for all birds wild
Just as he did when mother was a child.

Cinquain (traditional form): Windows

Brown eyes,
Bright and shining.
Let me see beauty there!
Your purpose, to reveal the soul
Within.

Clerihew: To a Fine Poet

To Scooter

My friend, I love your poems!
Bring out the jeroboams:
Let's drink some fine champagne
And read them over again.

Rondelet: To Precious Moments

Gold sands of time
Running through the hourglass. Fleeting,
Gold sands of time
Mark occasions when lovers chime
In time's fields of flowers. Meeting
'Ere we end—a joyous greeting!
Gold sands of time.

Triolet: My Father's Legacy

My darling father, may God rest his soul,
Showed me when dying that there's naught to fear:
His life, well lived with piety, was whole.
My darling father, may God rest his soul.
He loved us all, and saw that as his role;
He put us first, above his fine career.
My darling father, may God rest his soul,
Showed me when dying that there's naught to fear.

Tyburn: The Challenge of the Chase

Waiting,
Dating,
Mating,
Rating.
How I play'd that waiting, dating game.
I did love all that mating, rating same.

Tyburn: Recovery

Reeling,
Feeling,
Kneeling,
Healing.
Senses all are reeling, feeling bright.
Grateful, I am kneeling, healing Light!

Concrete: Can you see?

Oh
Look here!
What do I see?
I can see a lovely tree.
It is a Scottish pine, I vow.
It's a very fine tree, any old how.
Let's take it indoors and let's decorate it
With angel, tinsel, toys, lights, chocolate. It
Will look
So good
In a tub
Of wood.
Now, do
You see
My tree?

Concrete: Flying High

see
the balloon up in
the air, floating high into the
atmosphere, sailing over the furniture,
bobbing in the warm currents formed by our
breathing, as we blow it back and forth. Up and
down it dances! How long can it stay around,
swirling its rainbows round our living room?
I sometimes do wish that I could live in
in that lovely bubble, shielded from
harm, but I would not want
to have to go pop.
See?

Bandit Burmilla Babies

Helterskelter, fisticuffing, roly-poly,
Squeaking, skipping, getting stuck,
Mountaineering up the curtains,
Mewing with excitement,
Shouting, singing, smacking,
Sniffing. Upside down,
Their bottoms licked
By mother, Tui.
Waking up big brother, Magic
(Very dangerous proposition!)
Chasing tails and ambushing,
Eating something new and tasty,
Pingpong footballers, wheeee!
Growling, growing,
Ripping catnipped toys,
Racing, tumbling, jumping, surprised
By unfamiliar noises,
Suckling Tui's sweet warm milk,
Cud..dl...ing, purrrr.....ing
Dropp.......ing,
SNORING in a heap,
Fast asleep
(hush).
No wonder!
Little wonders.

Haiku: Night Scene in Manhattan

Reflecting starlight,
Illumination returns
From ev'ning's bright hearths

Haiku: Sacred Light

Satin silver moon;
Mystic goddess radiant
Shines from the heavens.

Haiku: Sunset Hymn

Light frames dark'ning cloud.
Angels at the end of day
Sing God's perfect words.

Rondeau: My Husband's Eyes

In my husband's dark brown eyes
Laughter, love, and joy arise.
He is my companion, hero,
Warmth, when the temperature is zero.
He's compassionate, strong, and wise.

I have come to realise
I have won the greatest prize
In the world, above, below,
In his dark eyes.

And so my heart leaps up and cries
A "thank you!" to the listening skies.
Wouldn't swap him for Juan Miro!
I, Columbine, see my Pierrot
(Whilst my heart to heaven flies)
In his dark eyes.

Haiku: Hidden in the Fir tree

Grey feathers trembling,
Heart beating, wings fluttering
Tiny bird. Praise be!

Triolet: Time gone by.

When I reflect on time gone by,
Good memories shine within my heart
And joy is evident to the eye,
When I reflect on time gone by.
I never dare to question why—
That might upset my applecart!
When I reflect on time gone by,
Good memories shine within my heart.

Three Than-Bauks

Misunderstood,
Don't feel good, so
I could be sad.

If I were sad,
That's real bad, and
I've had to change.

I see the signs:
Laughter lines! Look,
There shines a smile.

Statue of the Seated Buddha

In Vienna,
In the Mak Museum,
In the basement,
In the central
Oriental Collections room
I found him. Golden, serene,
Long-fingered hands resting upon his lap,
And his eyes, huge pools of wisdom;
His eyes, focused on infinity.
Oh, his eyes!
This Buddha was as a portal
To infinite consciousness.

I asked, "What do you see?
How does this world of ours look
From here in the basement,
From your eyes,
From your perspective,
From your enlightenment?"

He drew me in. I looked
Out of his eyes,
Out, from his consciousness,
Out, to infinity.
I laughed and I wept
And I gasped
With the beauty of it all,
With the pain of it all.
Not a shape was there,
Nothing differentiated.
All was one.
All was golden, all serene,
One vast pool
Of wisdom.

I whispered, "Is this really

How it is?"

Rondelet: My Darling Vicki

Generous heart,
Compassion is your guiding star.
Generous heart,
You bring great talent to your art—
No finer jeweller than you are,
(Well, possibly there's just one: JAR.),
Generous heart.

Sense of humour
Bubbling up, your bright eyes shining.
Sense of humour;
Sharing gossip, telling rumour
Whilst at Olivetto's dining.
Laughter, in between designing,
Sense of humour.

Villanelle: How time flies.

How time flies when you're having fun.
I don't believe that time can wait,
When everything is said and done.

We share a quip, invent a pun,
And suddenly, it's getting late.
How time flies when you're having fun.

It feels as if we've just begun!
It's no use getting in a state,
When everything is said and done

We'll only fret and come undone
(Not a good personality trait).
How time flies when you're having fun.

So tell your daughters (or your son)
Not to repeat this tiresome fate
When everything is said and done.

So have you lost, or have you won,
When you have played life's game till late?
How time flies when you're having fun,
When everything is said and done.

Ode to Maria Grachvogel

I am so proud of you, my friend.
When A-listers in your designs,
Looking so exquisite, attend
The Oscars, 'tis your dress that shines!

You do not care for Fashion's fuss,
The hype or glitz, for your pure vision
Is full of true integrity, thus
You plough your furrow with precision.

Beauty's ideal you manifest
With no regard for praise or taunt.
Your aim: to see all women dress'd
Confidently (then how we'll flaunt!).

Achieving this, you're also able
To run your House with charm and skill.
So young, you own a famous Label.
Dear friend, may you all dreams fulfil.

Haiku: Elephant Ride

Carried on your back
Safely to the Amber Fort.
Massive, ancient soul.

Sonnet: The Forces of Nature

A salmon swims upstream to procreate,
Driven by urge beyond the conscious mind.
The river's force denies this would-be mate
An easy path through waters so unkind.

The salmon's soul is constant, rivers change,
So never does it swim same waters twice.
The gleaming fish's body, just as strange,
Renews its atoms at the soul's advice.

38

And so renewed, the salmon swims the foam,
Opposes renewed water every Spring.
The fish's steady soul holds dreams of home
Tho' Earth her streams to the vast ocean bring.

The soul, for love and procreation yearning
Against all force, ensures its safe returning.

Magic's Song

I'm Magic!

I can bounce.

See?

Look at me!

Wheeee!

Boyng

boynnng

wheeeeeeeeee!

Joy am I.

the sky

is part of me

and I,

the sky,

Yaaay!

Earth,

my trampoline.

Look up,

up

into soft white,

bright

blue!

I bounce

from emerald lawn

to heaven's

embrace.

Yes.

The Ballad of St. Nicholas

In Patara was born a man
In two-hundred-sixty AD
Who lived according to God's plan.
A saintly man was he.

He grew in goodness and in light.
His generous heart earn'd fame.
He helped the poor by day and night,
And Nicholas was his name.

Three bags of gold to sisters three
He gave in secret, kind donation.
This to avert their poverty,
For their lives a firm foundation.

One stormy night his prayers went out
And mighty waves did calmly cease.
The sailors praised this man devout,
And knew his saintly words brought peace.

A bishop in Myra he became
And Emperor Diocletian knew
To spread God's word was Nicholas' aim,
And this was not a welcome view.

In dungeon dark some time he lay
Until another Emperor's reign.
Nicholas was freed without delay
In Holy Constantine's domain.

Nicholas died in Three-forty-three.
In Myra, according to his word,
His bones were buried—but now we see
In Bari, Italy, he's interred.

He's now the patron saint of brides,
Of innocent prisoners (no wrongdoers),
Of pawnbrokers, and more besides,
Of children, sailors, scholars, brewers.

Our Santa Claus of present day
Developed from this dear saint's story.
Washington Irving gave him a sleigh
So he could ride the skies in glory!

In America, Santa grew fat:
A cartoonist, one Thomas Nast,
Gave him a pipe and big furry hat.
Our Santa Claus was forming fast.

In nineteen thirty, a jolly Swede,
Haddon Sundblom, gave coat of red
And reindeer as his faithful steed,
And see, the modern legend's spread.

From Patara to Cola ad
Saint Nicholas' magic sheds its glow;
From generous saint to dressed-up dad,
From piety to "Ho, ho, ho!"

Spirit of winter, bountiful soul,
We watch for you through storms of snow;
We celebrate your Christmas role,
Noble and pious, your gifts o'erflow!

Senryu: The Mind Then the Word

In the beginning,
Before the Word, was the Thought
In the Mind of God.

Senryu: Possibilities

In the space between
Mind and body, there exists
Complete potential.

Abecedarian: Christmas Holiday Diary

Admired beautiful carols.
Did everyone favours gladly.
Happily, I just knew love more now.
Oh, popular quest!
Reverie sweet that understood
(Very well)
Xmas' yuletide zeal.

DHL Challenge

For Andreas and Vivienne

Your challenge to me was, "Now make up a rhyme
Of the DHL label in double quick time!"
So thank you, dear friends, for my wonderful, pleasant,
Colourful, comfortable Christmassy present:
A "Viv. Westwood" blanket—complete happiness—
And brought to me personally, DHL Express!
I read on the label, "Please do not send cash;"
Why? Does the great stress of it bring on a rash?
"Also, don't send cash equivalent or jewels."
We just wouldn't dream of it—we are no fools!
Of course I would not send large diamond collars.
"Liability shall not exceed a hundred US Dollars."
Thanks, Andreas, Vivienne. Your gift is just swell
And delivered so well by good ol' DHL.

Cherub in My Kitchen

A cherub flew into my kitchen today.
He was just passing by, and he wanted to say
That his work isn't easy. He brings love that is pure,
But whether we welcome it he isn't sure.

We say that we value the gift that he brings,
But continue to do the most terrible things.
He can't understand why we fight, kill, and maim.
He's heard all our reasons—they're always the same.

Lip service we pay to our God, who we vow
Is always supporting on our side. But how
Do we dare to assume that? The cherub gave sigh
And whispered, "I fear that your thoughts are awry."

I promised I'd tell you his message, my friends,
So that those with a good heart can make some amends.
He laughed and said hopefully, "Love is the key!
Believe with your hearts and your souls shall be free."

He fluttered his wings, played a tune on his lute,
Sang celestial songs, gave a loving salute.
Then he flew from my kitchen, leaving me to reflect
On the nature of humans, and of love and respect.

Parallelismus Membrorum: Slight Case of Ardour

You are annoyingly
Laid back and tranquil.
In this imperfect world
You are my ideal.
May I mutedly understate
My breathless adoration?
I cannot understand
How you're so wise!
Hate to confess,
But I love you.

Pantoum: Our Road to Damascus

Sometimes, in our routine lives,
We awake and are aware
Of something greater than ourselves,
Surrounding, supporting us with love.

We awake and are aware
There is a Deity benign,
Surrounding, supporting us with love.
Then we in turn reach out.

There is a Deity benign
Throughout time He existed, still exists.
Then we in turn reach out
And love flows one to another.

Throughout time He existed, still exists
In that divine dimnsion,
And love flows one to another
In a precious heartbeat.

In that divine dimension,
From routine lives awakened
In a precious heartbeat,
We experience the miracle of love.

Acrostic: Oh, Be My Valentine?

Only you I love, my sweet;
Hear my plea (but be discrete!)

Butterfly kisses on my cheek,
Eyes that sparkle, great physique!

Many shining moments, too—
You will have a love that's true.

Very special treats I bring.
At your window, hear me sing.
Longing for your favours now
Every day I raise my brow,
Never losing hope that you
Think of me and love me, too.
I will dream that we'll entwine.
Never falter, Valentine.
Ever more, wilt thou be mine?

A Southern African Legend

A lioness to a perfect cub gave birth,
Then went to hunt for food to feed her son.
She loved him so, was conscious of his worth
And grateful that his life had now begun.

His eyes still closed, he had not seen his mother.
A terrifying storm engulfed the cub.
He searched for her alone, he sought no other
Through lightning, thunder, all mayhem's hubbub.

At last, in meadow green, the cub was sighing,
"I want my Ma!" His cries were overheard
By a kind ewe: "I'll be your Ma. Stop crying."
The cub found solace in her kindly word.

So one day, when the lioness was seeking,
As she had done a long year, for her child,
She came upon a lion who was speaking
Just like a lamb, and she was quite beguiled.

"Oh, my dear son," she cried, "at last I've found you!"
But he shrank from her, bleated, and took fright.
"You are so handsome, with fine mane around you."
Now something stirred within, he knew was right.

"Baaa baaa?" he said, and followed this strange creature.
She led him to a lake and said, "Reflect.
Your true image is there. Reclaim your nature."
The lion roared at last, his voice perfect.

We often, like the lion cub, are frightened
And seek to go along society's ways.
Some never find their own voice. Unenlightened,
They live their lives unfocused, in a daze.

So, my sweet friend, take heed the lion's story.
Examine social norms, don't follow blind.
Assume your greatness, own your rightful glory,
Be faithful to your inner heart and mind.

Villanelle: A Winter Love Song

When the weather's bleak and dire
I hurry home out of the cold.
You have lit a welcoming fire.

So I wish for nothing higher
Than your love, to have and hold,
When the weather's bleak and dire.

46

You know how I do admire
You whose love does not grow old.
You have lit a welcoming fire.

You warm my heart and you inspire
With your wit and wisdom bold,
When the weather's bleak and dire.

Will people hear an angel choir
When our tale comes to be told?
You have lit a welcoming fire.

Of your sweet love I'll never tire.
Husband, I know I've struck gold.
When the weather's bleak and dire,
You have lit a welcoming fire.

Sonnet: A Falling Tree

The old zen question, "Does a falling tree
Within the deepest forest make a sound
If no one's there to hear?" is very key,
And points me to philosophy profound.

Are butterflies that frolic in the daylight
Still beautiful when no one's there to see?
And scent of roses still enrich dark night
When no one senses their perfumery?

For those who've never hoped, can hope exist?
And those constrain'd in fetters yet be free?
For those who've never loved, can Love persist?
May Spirit, not experienc'd, still be?

Yet God is here, was here, constant persistence
Created, with no witnesss, our existence.

Ogden Nash

I'm convinced it is just as I feared:
The style Ogden Nash pioneered
Is never used nowadays and so is in great danger of becoming all
but totally and completely disappeared—
However revered.

Kyrielle: There's Beauty

When all alone my way I wend,
When fortune's low, without a friend,
I'll sing harmonic melody,
There's beauty in this world for me.

There's beauty in diurnal chores.
There's beauty in or out of doors.
To God I sing out gratefully:
There's beauty in this world for me.

Although cruel winter's winds are cold,
Though sadnesses are manifold,
And though life's prone to tragedy,
There's beauty in this world for me.

As springtime's sun climbs in the sky
And lambs, foals, calfs go skipping by,
Earth wears her mantle prettily.
There's beauty in this world for me.

In summer oft we go away
To foreign lands for holiday.
Returning home, I fondly see
There's beauty in this world for me.

Come autumn, bronze gold leaves do fall,
And bounteous harvests we recall.
Abundant fruits we reap with glee.
There's beauty in this world for me.

So whether weather's cool or warm,
With simmering sun or glowering storm,
I love my life jubilantly.
There's beauty in this world for me.

Hospitalised

To Mum

Pale sweet
face
on crisp white
pillow
silky white hair newly washed
by caring hands
Will you stay
or leave?
Breath not breath
but ventilator
assisted.
Metamorphosis into
bionic
woman:
Love,
who gave me flesh.

Haiku: Spirit into Action

Magenta blossom
By sun illuminated.
Beauty manifests.

A Passion for Perfume

What music can compare
To perfume?
Come, I will create with you
A symphony of oils, essences
Evoking wild or long forgotten
Feelings.
Top notes spin off like fanfares
Turning heads,
Capturing hearts
In a heartbeat.
Middle notes carrying the melody
For hours,
And the base notes,
Ah, base notes resound,
And echo, echo,
Echo.
So potent is my perfume, you will smile,
As a baby, at the scent of mother's milk,
Smiles with recognition.
Let me tempt you with narcotic florals
Of pittasponum, night blooming jasmine, azalea,
Or violet leaf grown in cool shade
Of olive trees in Southern France,
Ylang ylang, flower of flowers,
From Madagascar,
Cardamon, the oldest spice,
Whose blue-streaked flowers, yellow tipp'd,
Bring its warm sweetness
From Malabar coast.
Black pepper's kiss awakes indifferent hearts
To love,
And ginger from Jamaica lends
Its oriental, sexy flair.
From Africa, the myrrh tree's resin
Is said to come from Horus' tears,
And ancient Indian sandalwood
Used in sacred ritual, lights
The soul's divinity;
Vanilla, orchid's cousin,
Is sumptuous,
Sensual.

All these and more will I blend and bring,
And your heart will sing
To my perfumed symphony.

Villanelle: If We Could Talk with the Animals

For my dear friend Amelia Kinkade, the celebrated animal communicator

Your friendship warms my heart and soul,
To you I will take off my hat.
Amelia, you're rock'n'roll!

Your psychic gifts I do extol,
Your miracles I wonder at.
Your friendship warms my heart and soul.

You talk with horse, dog, goat, or foal,
With elephant or tiny gnat.
Amelia, you're rock'n'roll!

The shyest creatures you cajole,
The boldest just enjoy the chat.
Your friendship warms my heart and soul.

Come, let us share a drinking bowl
And reminisce on this and that.
Amelia, you're rock'n'roll!

Nobody else can fill your role—
Don't take my word, just ask my cat.
Your friendship warms my heart and soul,
Amelia, you're rock'n'roll!

Sonnet, Italian style: Orchid

As, when the sun does reach to heaven's height,
The sweet perfuméd orchid opens wide,
Inviting in Apollo's light with pride,
Reflecting iridescent colours bright,
So I, responding to my loving knight,
Open my heart, though vulnerable, with joy.
See how I trust you, brave companion boy,
Whose ardour's heat turns darkness into light.
And so, Beloved, should you stay by me,
Should you accept this flower, this my life,
You'll not know sorrow. I shall constant be,
And bring you peace and laughter, never strife.
I'll honour you with my soul's poetry
And be forever your devoted wife.

Sonnet: The Look of Love

You are my sublime meditation mantra;
Your face is ever in my heart and mind.
Love's sweet delights with you are more than tantra.
With eyes wide open, our love's never blind.
You lead me tenderly to hearts' true meeting;
Enraptur'd I, who thrills beneath your touch
And loves to hear your voice and merry greeting.
I am so bless'd; I love you, oh, so much!
As I reflect in silent contemplation
How you, my soulmate, lighten up my years,
In gratitude, in evening meditation,
I offer up a prayer, with blissful tears.
I visualise your likeness, love's encription,
And celebrate your shining soul's description.

Haiku: Grey, White Bird in Grey, White Sky

Seagull's silent flight,
Aerodynamics perfect,
Lifted by God's hand.

Grown-Up Nursery Rhyme

What care I, in a coat of blue?
Today I'll meet my lover true.
Diddle doddle diddle, diddledie do.

What care I, in a dress of yellow?
I'll give him kisses, the lovely fellow.
Pibble pobble pibble, pibbledie pillow.

What care I, in a hat of white?
I'll roger him all through the night.
Nibble nobble nibble, nibble delight.

What care I, in knickers of red?
I'll give him breakfast tea in bed.
Hibble hobble hibble, hibbledie head.

What care I, in my high-heeled shoesies?
I'm one of those brazen hussy-floozies!
Wiggle waggle wiggle, wiggledie woosies.

Sonnet: You Light My Fire

When blizzards chill us right into the bone
And rain and hail numb fingers through our glove,
I'm cozy as a queen upon a throne
Because you warm my heart, my dearest love.
However winter, fierce, forbidding, tries
To cool emotions, he will not succeed;
For in your arms there's strength, and in your eyes

Passion's hot fire burns very bright indeed.
So bring on all the storms winter can muster!
I'm safe within our home and warm as toast.
The furious tempests, all that raging bluster,
Just snuggles us together—Love's the Most!
The wild and savage weather gives good reasons
To welcome winter, happiest of seasons.

Haiku: In a Summer Garden

Bumble bees buzz round
Velvet blue petals, giving
Sweet, perfum'd honey.

Ode to a Pigeon

After a storm, a pigeon small
Appeared upon my sill, all huddled
In a corner, by the wall.
A homing bird was he, but muddled!

He had been blown away off course.
He was distressed, lost, hungry, cold.
The storm had raged with such fierce force.
He was a sad sight to behold.

I met his bright eyes through the pane
And straight in love with him I fell.
This scruffy bird, shelt'ring from rain,
Had captured me within his spell.

Oh he was brave, no shrinking coward,
He had flown far throughout the land.
I gave him seeds, which he devoured,
Then gradually he touched my hand.

He danced for me his pretty dance
With fanning wings and tail displayed;
He sang, "Crrrooo crrrooo!" with shining glance,
And for the next few weeks we played,

Until one day he came no more
To sit upon my windowsill.
That little bird yet I adore
And hold his memory with me still.

Haiku: Riches

Under autumn sun
Golden corn sheafs ripening.
Earth is bounteous.

Haiku: At the Day's End

Softly the ev'ning
Gath'ring mists around her skirts
Hails golden sunset.

A Question for the Hunter

Shiny as lacquer, each hair of your fur
Sparkles with health, and the sound of your purr
Is deafening me as you cuddle up close
To lighten my mood if I'm feeling morose.
Your ivory coat tipped with chocolate shade,
Your huge golden eyes tinged with green—God's displayed
His artistry here. I'm delighted you're mine
(Though I don't possess you.) I think you're divine
And thoroughly glad that you're sharing our house
But: Why did you torture that poor little mouse?

Making a Meal of It

Crudités, fresh, piled high and swaggering
From the market, bought this evening.
Thrusting carrots, earth still clinging,
Crisp cos, perky peppers, piquant roquette,
Rude red radishes, cucumber firm,
All in cool clear water washed,
Droplets sparkling on their surface.
Want to dip them in my hummus?

Temptresses teasing, to whet the appetite:
Oval curves unending, singing:
"Start with me." *Oeufs en cocotte*,
Yellow yolked white winking coquettes,
Lovely lazy daisies, out of work, *hors d'oeuvres*,
Swoon to your eager spoon.

Taking a breath, your mouth's alluring smile,
Eyes meet, hands connect,
Hot and cold shivers thrill.
An *amuse-bouche*:
Burning ginger flavours a cool sorbet.

How d'you like your steak, sir?
Rare, seared, visceral, red,
Caressed with oyster mushrooms wild,
Crushed peppercorns, randy brandy
Added accents to saucily seduce the palate,
Juliennes strewn prettily around the rim.

Velvet to the tongue,
Come, taste my peaches,
As moist flesh yields sweet warm juices
Merging flavours with wanton,
Whipped, drifting, dreamy, creamy domes.

Stimulation of the mocha and the mysore beans
Offering their perfume to enchant the air
As we sip, laugh, talk, and glance,
Flirt, flirt, and flirt.

Haiku: Where's the Action?

Two baby otters,
Shiny fur coats, eyes sparkling.
Alert for mischief.

Haiku: Flight from Hunters

Fallow foal, anxious,
Flees through the snowy forest.
Seeks his mother's warmth.

Haiku: Reunited

Pulse racing, eyes closed,
Breathless foal snuggles
With his mother, safe.

Interlocking Rubáiyát: The Wonderful Wizard

Have you heard the story "The Wizard Of Oz"?
A wonderful wizard they said that he was,
But all that he was, was a travelling man.
No hero, no magical guy, he had flaws.

However, he reckoned that since time began,
We all needed miracles in our life's plan,
And so when four characters came to his place
He said, "Do these difficult tasks, if you can!"

They accomplished his missions with ease and with grace.
The wizard rewarded them all, face to face.
Each one wished for something they already had,
So their prizes were fun to award and embrace.

The Scarecrow, who thought that a brain he might add,
Was most intellectual, the cleverest lad.
The Tin Man, who was most compassionate of all,
Believed he had no heart, and that made him sad.

The lion, who thought that his courage was small,
Was the one who eventually won every brawl.
And Dorothy, wanting to get her home back,
Knew there's no place like it, with the wisdom of Saul.

The wizard acknowledged their gifts (though a quack),
Then each one could recognise they did not lack
Their attributes, which were abundant inside,
And this gave them all a tremendous great craic.

So believe, when your light under bushels you hide,
And to gurus you turn, seeking some wise old guide,
Find your wisdom within and let that be your cause.
Or, like Dorothy, click those red heels side to side!

Love's Amplitudes

Rollicking love,
Shouting, frollicking love,
Love that erupts in laughter
At the startle and relief of meeting;
Delight of touching, tasting;
Feel like yelling, "I adore you!"
Loud love, massive,
Love from mountain tops blaring;
Abracadabra!
All this world I saw before
But did not see,
Not so heightened, so intensely beautiful,
So completely realised.
Now the colourness, soundness,
Bounteousness, connectedness,
Coming-homeness
Explodes like Guy Fawkes Night—
All bonfires, roman candles,
Sparklers, and parkin—
In my grateful, dancing, welcoming heart.
Great, magic love.

Gentle love,
Sensitive, remembering love,
So full of reflections, happiness, and sorrow.
Celebrating, sharing, your strong arms around me.
The good woollen scent of your jumper
As I lay my head on your shoulder,
How I love your bright brown eyes,
Laughter lines a tribute to our happiness.
Quiet love, reposing now.
Nurturing, offering sanctuary,
Accepting, attentive love.
Peacefulness, tenderness,
Contentedness, oneness
Settles as a white turtledove
Fluttering feathers, nestling,
Silently smiling in my heart.
Perfect, sacred love.

Haiku: To the Summit

The ibex, agile,
Confident and sure of foot,
On his path ascends.

Parking Fine Valentine

Caution:
Do not attempt to remove yourself.
You have incurred the penalty
Of my undying devotion.
My heart and soul are clamped to yours;
Removal could mean a huge fine.
You are so fine, I find.
Get your engine in gear and accompany me.
Give me ideas above my station.
You have been found
Obstructing my peace of mind.
I may just tow you home,
Bumper to bumper,
And let you park your chassis
Really close to mine.
My fine
Valentine.

Sonnet: On an Ankle Injury

"Bugger!" I thought, as I felt the tendons rip.
I should have looked with care where I was going.
The last thing that I needed on this trip
Was a busted ankle. See, the swelling's growing!
My friends realised the injury was dire
When I gave away my pass to Dior's show.
Imagine the extent of my self-ire?
I do admit it, that was quite a blow.

Returning to my room, then ambulance
By doctor summoned straight to "A & E."
'Twill be a while from now before I dance.
I'm feeling very sorry now for me.
I wore flat boots, not usual four inch heel.
Ironic and inconvenient, I feel.

Haiku: Before Germination

In winter the earth,
Snow cover'd, molten at heart,
Cares for sleeping seeds.

Morning

Subtle caress of dawning's yellow light
Accentuates the landscape;
In the day's beginning, hope and joy embrace:
There's opulence here.
I stretch open my arms to infinite bliss,
To full, white, heady blossoms in laughing bouquet.
Mine is this day, to do with as I please.
Each mindful moment moves me
To the beat of my heart,
To the centre of my soul.
Wild, bold, glorious imaginings now manifest.
A blackbird soars,
His delirious song erupting
Into the welcoming air.
My stalwart friend the sun climbs heaven high
And warms to my purpose.
Beauty of creation, splendid, shining
In the eyes of my love,
Permeates my existence.
Dear God!
Praise be for this morning
At one with You.

Haiku: In the Beginning

Glistening serpent
Gliding, slithering, curling
Wisdom's harbinger.

Wind Voyager

So feather light is my soul today
That one kind breath of a word from you
Sends me flurrying high with the breeze,
Carrying, extolling Creation's mystic secret,
As the golden dandelion
Entrusts her children to the billowing, willow swaying zephyrs.

I yield to the wonder of the wind's warm caress,
My love pirouetting toward you,
Inexorably, supporting my glad heart's intention
To grow tall and strong, to thrive
Within your rich, welcoming, earthy
Abundance.

Sonnet: Guardian Angel

Just as the swan, with her balletic grace,
Floating in peace o'er lazuline blue lake,
Shields cygnets in her motherly embrace,
So does my angel perfect haven make.
He wraps me in his feather'd wings of love,
And nourishes me when life seems awry;
When conflict harsh strikes like a dueling glove,
He with protection answers to my cry.
In joy he aids my soul's sure evolution,
Teaching celestial hymns of piety,
With blessings offers me his contribution,
And in compassion's name he sets me free.
His care pervades my earthly life's material,
So perfect is his guardianship ethereal.

Sonnet: On a Detail in a François Boucher Painting

Poems ascend in luminous sapphire skies
As prettily as any Boucher dove
In flight eternal. Artist's strokes devise
Each beauteous form to represent great love.
How many shades of light, how many hues,
Playfully linger on each feathery wing?
Such subtle shadows! Gentle tones infuse
The senses, sweetly prompt the soul to sing.
Cherubs frolic, blissful, plump, and pink,
Companions to each poem or lovely bird,
Painted in Master's oils, or pen and ink,
They celebrate that now their song is heard.
Once seen, once read, no one can rend asunder
These artefacts portraying Nature's wonder.

Sonnet: Hymn to the Animals

The eagle soars, his strong wings beat the air,
His eyes are focused high in cloudless skies.
How else can that great bird create a prayer
Than flight, wherein his joyous thoughts arise.
The fox and vixen frolic in the lea,
Softly small firefly in dark meadow glows,
A squirrel scurries homeward to her tree,
A bumble bee sings praises to a rose.
All creatures have connection to the earth
And also to the azure heavens bright.
They sense the sacred Oneness from their birth
Emerging into life with pure delight.
Observing this, no wonder my heart's attitude
Is full of love, hope, piety, and gratitude.

Haiku: Migration Time

Each bird flies within
His soaring flock of brothers,
Southward to the sun.

65

Haiku: Elemental Bliss

Solitude, dreaming,
Reflections of the ocean
Clouds and waves entwine.

Love Moves Softly

Love moves softly with a delicate grace,
Enriching my profound desire like summer blossoms
Strewn upon the white crested seas,
Wind kissed, which swell in lusty bloom.
The ocean with sometime gentle ebbs and flows
And sometime high crescendos
Serves the mistress moon;
Honeysuckle, jasmine, gardenia, rose
Swirl upon the laughing waves in dance,
Their fragrance dreamy, heady, dazzling-sweet,
Presenting scented beauty, as a rich incense,
O'er my heart's devotion and love's power immense.

Sonnet: The Antique Fan

Today I bought a pretty, antique fan.
It will be quite a star in my collection.
In eighteen sixty, when its life began,
Who was enthralled to own its sweet perfection?
Garlands and songbirds, set in mother-o'-pearl,
Hold delicate lovers: shepherd, shepherdess.
See, cupid aims his darts at boy and girl
Captured, enraptured, in love's first caress.
What lady held it first close to her cheek
To cool her rosy blush when she was shy?
And did she dream of love she could not speak,
Flutt'ring this fan to catch her lover's eye?
Today's women are bold. We tell emotions.
Lost is all subtlety of romantic notions.

Sonnet: Beyond, Behind, Before, Above.

Beyond the bright'ning stars, further than moon
And planets, is the Universal Mind;
Behind manifestation there are strewn
Existence-cosmic templates, intertwined
Pattern on pattern, potential lives on lives,
Precursors sacred in Immortal Plan.
Before a thing exists, becomes, and thrives,
As thund'ring mountain, mighty ocean, man,
Before the tiny flower, worm, or fly
Is made reality, there is The Thought,
(Vision ethereal of Creation's eye)
'Ere matter physical is robustly wrought.
So much beyond, behind, before, above
All life, and I can gladly call it Love.

Swan Song

The shaman in Siberian snows,
Singing and dying
And flying;
The Gnostic in life creating lines
Of song, of death,
Learning to heart his poetry,
To sing
With his last breath;
Pythagorus's sacred password verse
Easing his transition
To heaven
From earth;
All know the deep wisdom
Of the mystic swan
Who sings as her soul takes flight
Towards the Love,
Towards the Light.

By the power of song,
By lines of love,
By pure poetry and profound enchantment,

We embrace the joyful journey
To the world
Of Spirit.

Clogyrnach: Ray Brown and Paul of Tarsus

Last week, a psychic surgeon, Ray,
Healed folk in trance—a great display.
He brought through St. Paul
Who then healed them all.
I'm in thrall,
Blown away!

Two thousand years ago was when
He walked on earth with mortal men.
He now works to heal
And Truth to reveal:
Spirit's real.
Sing amen.

My love, return!

Delicious love poems and twilight,
Poppy fields, silent stars, and candlelight
Are better than falling teardrops,
My love.
Return to me!
The eagle's wings
Caress the embracing air
As he flies home.
Return to me!
I am listening, waiting
Under silent stars
For your return
And your blissful
Touch.
Here's candlelight to guide you to my door,
And poppies sweet in bed to give you lullaby.
Return to me
To warm my heart with laughter
And find repose,
My love.

An Incident
7th July 2005

A London Transport employee,
wearing a waterproof, fluorescent yellow,
company jacket,
turned me away
at the gates to
East Finchley Underground
Station.
"An incident, Madam,
or a possible power surge
on the line.
There are casualties.
The Service is suspended."

In the station forecourt
crowds of people
are trying to contact
people
on their phones,
to no avail.
Mobile networks
shut down for fear
Of triggering more
bombs.

Later, back home,
family, friends, clients,
and folk we had not heard from
for many,
many
years
are calling, saying,
"You OK? Were you hurt?
We love you. We could not
bear the thought
of losing
you.
Keep safe! Keep safe!
You're in our thoughts."

Had I not procrastinated,
picked up e-mails, fed the cats,
made phone calls,
my proposed journey
into Knightsbridge
by Piccadilly Line
would have been
my last.

I grieve for the victims
of the rabid
terrorist, full of
hatred,
who feels justified
in barbaric acts
of carnage.
I grieve also
for the victims
of official, governmental,
orchestrated terror
in lands far away.
Sometimes it's hard
to be optimistic
about the progress
of the human soul,
isn't
it.

I give thanks to God
that I did not
die
today.

Interlocking Rubáiyát: Man's Inhumanity to Man

Man's inhumanity to Man
Transmits beyond a lifetime's span,
Flows, abusive, from generation
To generation, since the world began.

This is my sorrowful observation:
We must call halt, else all creation

Will subject be to violence dread,
Shaken to the core foundation.

I advocate we strive instead
To help each other, share our bread
With those less fortunate. Let us seek
To heal life's wounds and forge ahead.

The earth, inherited by the meek,
Shall bring forth fruit for all who speak
Of love instead of hate or fear,
For love does own a power unique.

So with great awe let all draw near
On this bright day. Let's start from here:
Let sacred healing be our plan.
Then hope for Man shall reappear.

Sing to Us of Gentleness

Blessed Creator
Of history's eternally reflecting colours,
Retell to us the infinite newness
And dazzle of love.
Remind us of the brilliance
Of adoration, and the truth and hope
That daily, as the newborn child,
Emerges bringing clarity
To our obscured realities.
How misty do exhausted souls become,
Too weary when the call goes forth
To stand up and be counted?
When one to a brother does great harm,
Calling him enemy,
Assuming Your allegiance.
Remind us that we to ourselves do harm
In that dread warlike action.
Sing to us of gentleness
And compassionate deeds
That we with harmony can redress
And heal the wounds
Of our thoughtlessness.

Sonnet: Psalm

Sunlight illuminates my upturned face
And Heaven's presence overwhelms my heart.
Now all of life is mindful of that grace
That flowed throughout Creation from the start.
In gratitude I celebrate this day;
In admiration dedicate my soul;
In hopefulness with hymns supplicant, pray
To You who can restore and make me whole.
All vivid colours, wondrous scents and sounds,
All welcome meals or loved one's tender kiss,
Show how Your generosity abounds
To heighten our awareness and our bliss.
My being is a spark of Your divinity
So I embrace with joy Your pure infinity.

Haiku: Vermillion Evening

The sky, flame colour'd,
Lights the ending of the day
With soul-bright sunset.

Lightning Source UK Ltd.
Milton Keynes UK
07 September 2009

143434UK00002B/43/P